Best-Loved Hymns

ARRANGED BY *Dan Fox*

Contents

2 Abide With Me
3 Amazing Grace
4 Beneath The Cross Of Jesus
5 Christ The Lord Is Risen Today
6 Church In The Wildwood, The
8 Church's One Foundation, The
9 Come, Thou Almighty King
10 Crown Him With Many Crowns
11 Fairest Lord Jesus
12 Faith Of Our Fathers, Living Still
14 God Of Our Fathers Whose Almighty Hand
15 He Leadeth Me, O Blessed Thought
16 Holy, Holy, Holy! Lord God Almighty
17 I Need Thee Every Hour
18 In The Sweet Bye And Bye
20 It Is Well With My Soul
22 Just A Closer Walk With Thee
19 Just As I Am Without One Plea
24 Lead On, O King Eternal
25 Mighty Fortress Is Our God, A
26 My Jesus, I Love Thee
27 Nearer, My God, To Thee
28 Now Thank We All Our God
29 O For A Thousand Tongues To Sing
30 O God, Our Help In Ages Past
32 Onward, Christian Soldiers
31 Praise God From Whom All Blessings Flow
34 Praise To The Lord, The Almighty
36 Precious Memories
38 Rock Of Ages, Cleft For Me
40 Shall We Gather At The River?
39 Sweet Hour Of Prayer
42 Take My Life And Let It Be
43 We Gather Together To Ask The Lord's Blessing
44 Were You There?
45 When I Survey The Wondrous Cross
46 Whispering Hope

Cover photo: Roger Markham Smith

HAL•LEONARD®
CORPORATION

7777 W. BLUEMOUND RD. P.O. BOX 13819 MILWAUKEE, WI 53213

Copyright © 1986 HAL LEONARD PUBLISHING CORPORATION
International Copyright Secured   ALL RIGHTS RESERVED   Printed in the U.S.A.
For all works contained herein:
Unauthorized copying, arranging, adapting, recording or public performance is an infringement of copyright.
Infringers are liable under the law.

ABIDE WITH ME

Copyright © 1986 HAL LEONARD PUBLISHING CORPORATION
International Copyright Secured   ALL RIGHTS RESERVED   Printed in the U.S.A.

AMAZING GRACE

Moderately

Copyright © 1986 HAL LEONARD PUBLISHING CORPORATION
International Copyright Secured   ALL RIGHTS RESERVED   Printed in the U.S.A.

BENEATH THE CROSS OF JESUS

Be - neath the cross of Je - sus I fain would take my stand, The shad - ow of a might - y rock with - in a wear - y land, A home with - in the wil - der - ness, a rest up - on the way, From the burn - ing of the noon - tide heat and the bur - den of the day.

Copyright © 1986 HAL LEONARD PUBLISHING CORPORATION
International Copyright Secured   ALL RIGHTS RESERVED   Printed in the U.S.A.

CHRIST THE LORD IS RISEN TODAY

Copyright © 1986 HAL LEONARD PUBLISHING CORPORATION
International Copyright Secured   ALL RIGHTS RESERVED   Printed in the U.S.A.

THE CHURCH IN THE WILDWOOD

Moderate steady beat

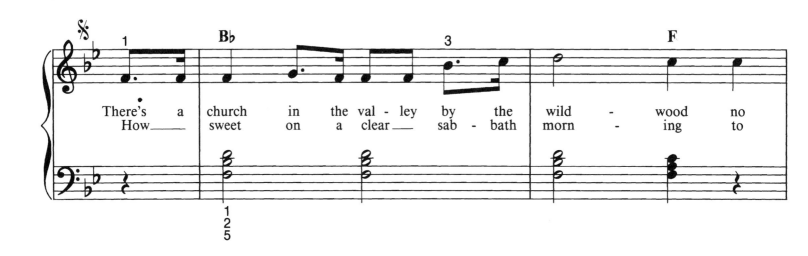

There's a church in the val - ley by the wild - wood no

How____ sweet on a clear____ sab - bath morn - ing to

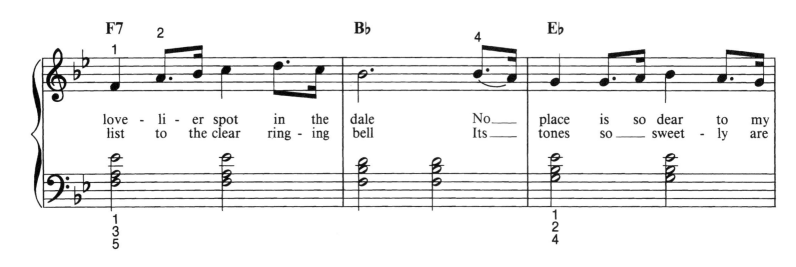

love - li - er spot in the dale

list to the clear ring - ing bell

No____ place is so dear to my

Its____ tones so ____ sweet - ly are

Copyright © 1986 HAL LEONARD PUBLISHING CORPORATION
International Copyright Secured   ALL RIGHTS RESERVED   Printed in the U.S.A.

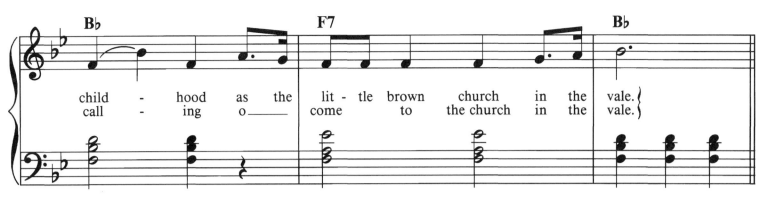

child - hood as the lit - tle brown church in the vale.
call - ing o come to the church in the vale.

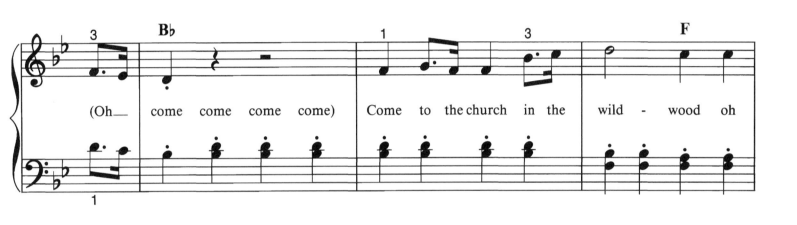

(Oh come come come come) Come to the church in the wild - wood oh

come to the church in the vale! No place is so dear to my

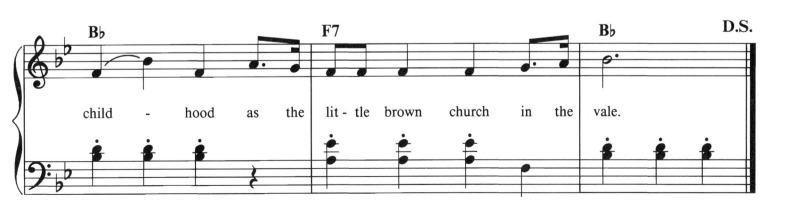

child - hood as the lit - tle brown church in the vale.

THE CHURCH'S ONE FOUNDATION

The Chur-ch's one Foun-da - tion is Je-sus Christ, her Lord. She is His new cre-a - tion by wa-ter and the word. From heav'n He came and sought her to be His ho-ly Bride; With His own blood He bought her, And for her life He died.

Copyright © 1986 HAL LEONARD PUBLISHING CORPORATION
International Copyright Secured   ALL RIGHTS RESERVED   Printed in the U.S.A

COME, THOU ALMIGHTY KING

Copyright © 1986 HAL LEONARD PUBLISHING CORPORATION
International Copyright Secured   ALL RIGHTS RESERVED   Printed in the U.S.A.

CROWN HIM WITH MANY CROWNS

Copyright © 1986 HAL LEONARD PUBLISHING CORPORATION
International Copyright Secured   ALL RIGHTS RESERVED   Printed in the U.S.A.

FAIREST LORD JESUS

Copyright © 1986 HAL LEONARD PUBLISHING CORPORATION
International Copyright Secured   ALL RIGHTS RESERVED   Printed in the U.S.A.

FAITH OF OUR FATHERS, LIVING STILL

Moderately

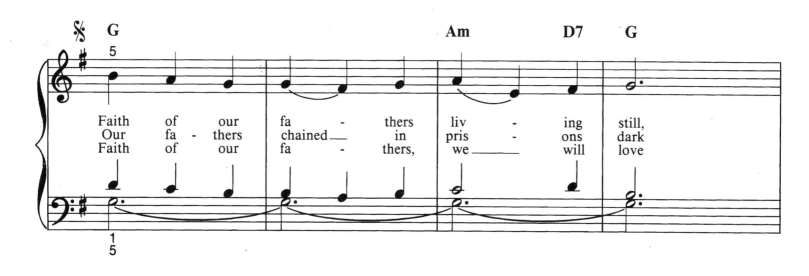

Faith of our fa - thers, liv - ing still,
Our fa - thers chained in pris - ons dark
Faith of our fa - thers, we will love

In spite of dun - geon fire and sword.
Were still in heart and con - science free.
Both friend and foe in all our strife.

Copyright © 1986 HAL LEONARD PUBLISHING CORPORATION
International Copyright Secured   ALL RIGHTS RESERVED   Printed in the U.S.A.

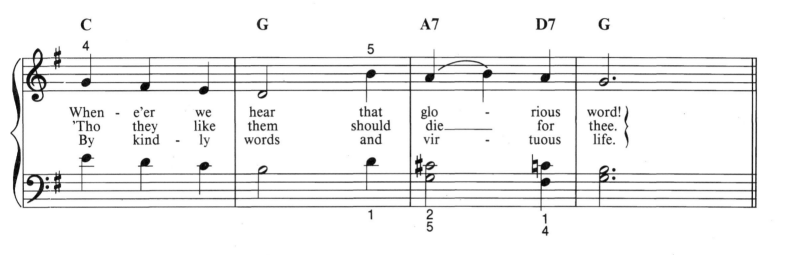

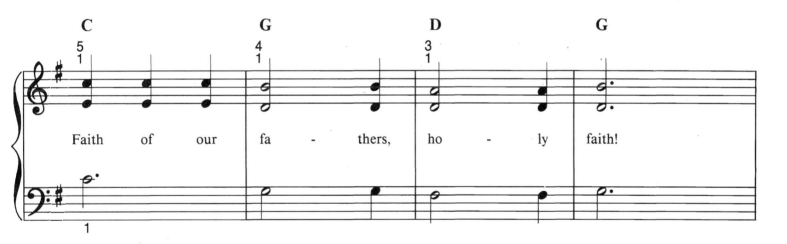

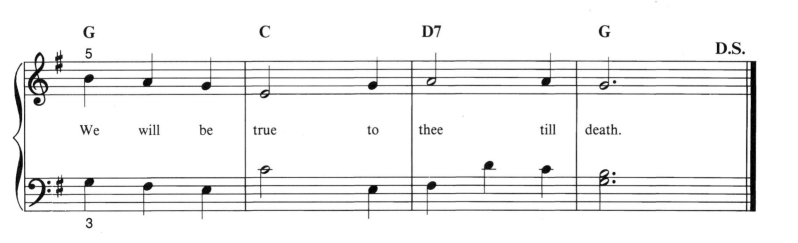

GOD OF OUR FATHERS WHOSE ALMIGHTY HAND

God of our fa - thers, whose al - might - y hand

Leads forth in beau - ty all the star - ry band

Of shin - ing worlds in splen - dor thro' the skies,

Our grate - ful songs be - fore thy throne a - rise.

Copyright © 1986 HAL LEONARD PUBLISHING CORPORATION
International Copyright Secured   ALL RIGHTS RESERVED   Printed in the U.S.A

HE LEADETH ME,
O BLESSED THOUGHT

Copyright © 1986 HAL LEONARD PUBLISHING CORPORATION
International Copyright Secured   ALL RIGHTS RESERVED   Printed in the U.S.A.

HOLY, HOLY, HOLY! LORD GOD ALMIGHTY

Copyright © 1986 HAL LEONARD PUBLISHING CORPORATION
International Copyright Secured   ALL RIGHTS RESERVED   Printed in the U.S.A.

I NEED THEE EVERY HOUR

Copyright © 1986 HAL LEONARD PUBLISHING CORPORATION
International Copyright Secured   ALL RIGHTS RESERVED   Printed in the U.S.A.

IN THE SWEET BYE AND BYE

Copyright © 1986 HAL LEONARD PUBLISHING CORPORATION
International Copyright Secured   ALL RIGHTS RESERVED   Printed in the U.S.A.

JUST AS I AM WITHOUT ONE PLEA

Just — as — I am — with - out — one plea, But
Just — as — I am — tho' tossed — a - bout, With

that — Thy blood was shed for me, And — that Thou
man - y a con - flict, many a doubt, Fight - ings Thou and

bidd'st — me come, to Thee, — O Lamb of
fears — with - in, with - out, —

God, — I come! I come! —

Copyright © 1986 HAL LEONARD PUBLISHING CORPORATION
International Copyright Secured   ALL RIGHTS RESERVED   Printed in the U.S.A

IT IS WELL WITH MY SOUL

Copyright © 1986 HAL LEONARD PUBLISHING CORPORATION
International Copyright Secured   ALL RIGHTS RESERVED   Printed in the U.S.A.

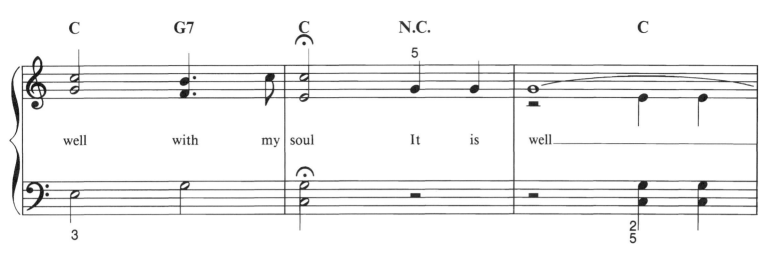

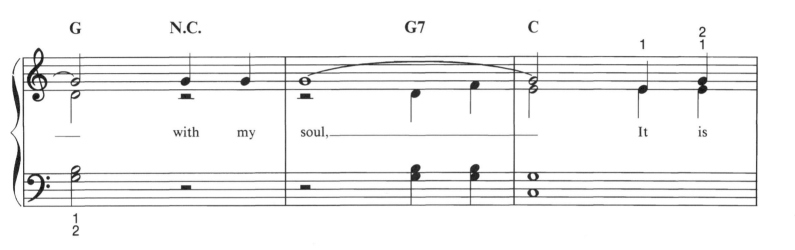

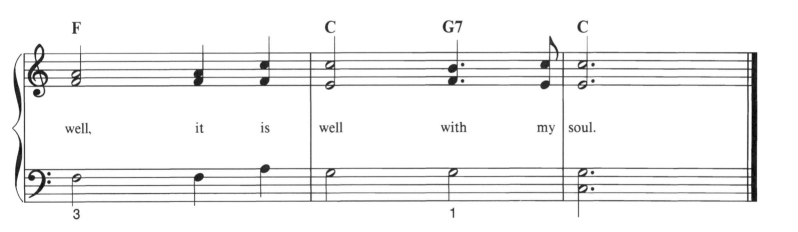

2. Though Satan should buffet, tho' trials should come,
   Let this blest assurance control,
   That Christ has regarded my helpless estate,
   And hath shed His own blood for my soul.

Chorus

3. My sin oh, the bliss of this glorious tho't
   My sin not in part, but the whole
   Is nailed to the cross and I bear it no more,
   Praise the Lord, praise the Lord, O my soul!

Chorus

4. And, Lord, haste the day when the faith shall be sight,
   The clouds be rolled back as a scroll,
   The trump shall resound and the Lord shall descend,
   "Even so" it is well with my soul.

Chorus

JUST A CLOSER WALK WITH THEE

Copyright © 1986 HAL LEONARD PUBLISHING CORPORATION
International Copyright Secured   ALL RIGHTS RESERVED   Printed in the U.S.A.

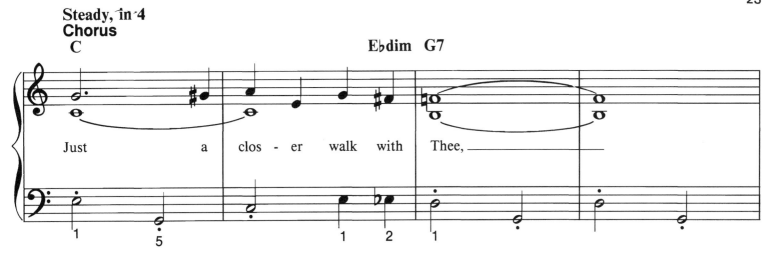

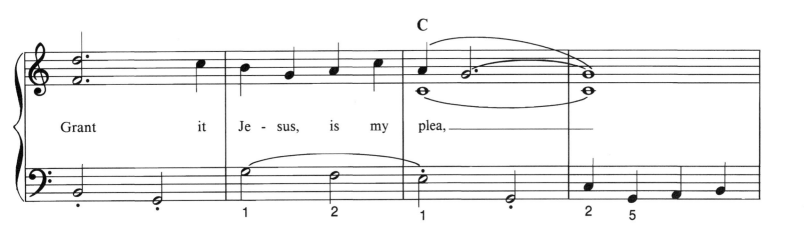

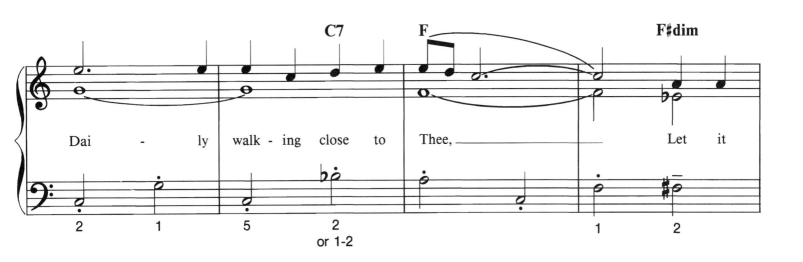

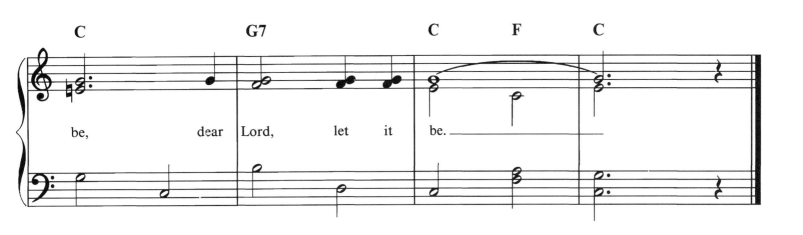

LEAD ON, O KING ETERNAL

Copyright © 1986 HAL LEONARD PUBLISHING CORPORATION
International Copyright Secured   ALL RIGHTS RESERVED   Printed in the U.S.A.

A MIGHTY FORTRESS IS OUR GOD

Copyright © 1986 HAL LEONARD PUBLISHING CORPORATION
International Copyright Secured   ALL RIGHTS RESERVED   Printed in the U.S.A.

MY JESUS, I LOVE THEE

Copyright © 1986 HAL LEONARD PUBLISHING CORPORATION
International Copyright Secured   ALL RIGHTS RESERVED   Printed in the U.S.A.

NEARER, MY GOD, TO THEE

Copyright © 1986 HAL LEONARD PUBLISHING CORPORATION
International Copyright Secured   ALL RIGHTS RESERVED   Printed in the U.S.A.

NOW THANK WE ALL OUR GOD

Copyright © 1986 HAL LEONARD PUBLISHING CORPORATION
International Copyright Secured   ALL RIGHTS RESERVED   Printed in the U.S.A.

O FOR A THOUSAND TONGUES TO SING

Moderately

O / Je- for a thou- sand tongues to sing, My great Re-deem-er's praise, The / sus! The name that charms our fears, That bids our sor-rows cease, 'Tis

glo- ries of my God and King, The__ tri-umphs of His grace! My / mus- ic in the sin- ners' ears 'Tis__ life and health and peace. He

gra- cious Mas- ter and my God, As- sist me to pro- claim, To / breaks the pow'r of can- celed sin, He sets the pris- 'ner free, His

spread thru' all the earth a- broad, The__ hon- ors of Thy name. / blood can make the foul- est clean, His__ blood a- vailed for me.

Copyright © 1986 HAL LEONARD PUBLISHING CORPORATION
International Copyright Secured   ALL RIGHTS RESERVED   Printed in the U.S.A.

O GOD, OUR HELP IN AGES PAST

Copyright © 1986 HAL LEONARD PUBLISHING CORPORATION
International Copyright Secured   ALL RIGHTS RESERVED   Printed in the U.S.A.

PRAISE GOD FROM WHOM ALL BLESSINGS FLOW

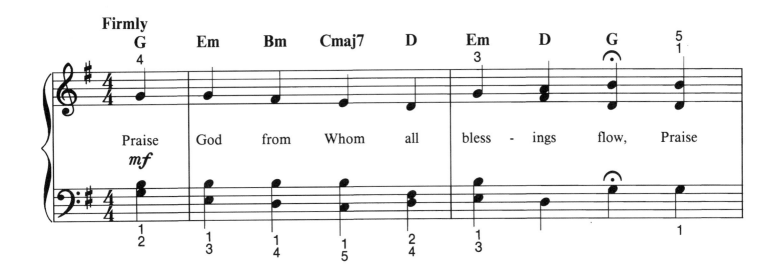

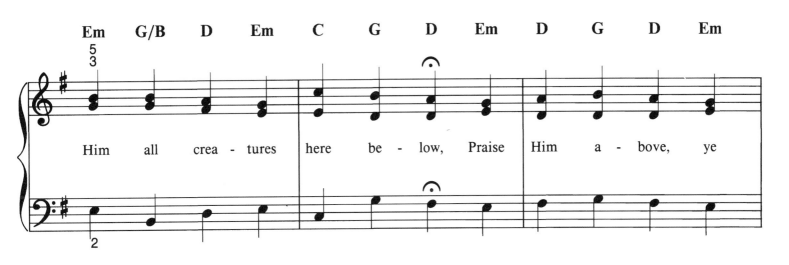

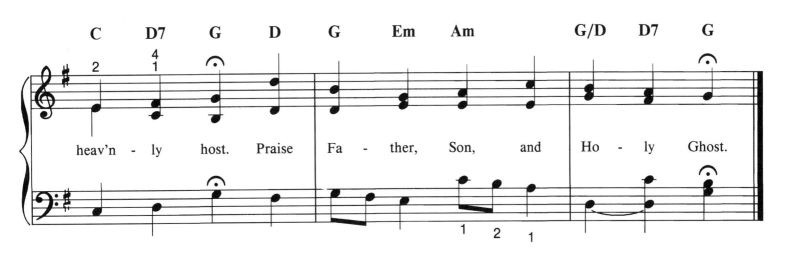

Copyright © 1986 HAL LEONARD PUBLISHING CORPORATION
International Copyright Secured   ALL RIGHTS RESERVED   Printed in the U.S.A.

ONWARD, CHRISTIAN SOLDIERS

Like a slow march

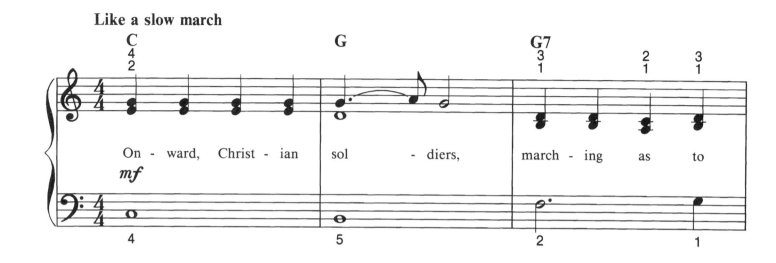

On - ward, Christ - ian sol - diers, march - ing as to

mf

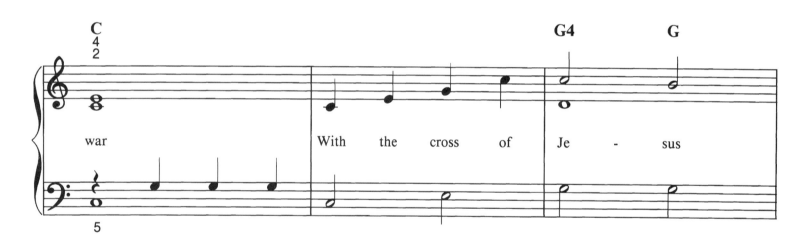

war   With the cross of Je - sus

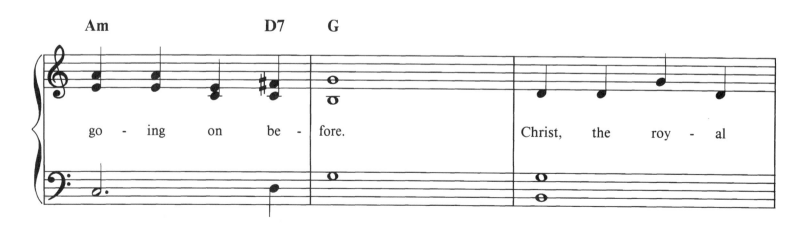

go - ing on be - fore.   Christ, the roy - al

Copyright © 1986 HAL LEONARD PUBLISHING CORPORATION
International Copyright Secured   ALL RIGHTS RESERVED   Printed in the U.S.A.

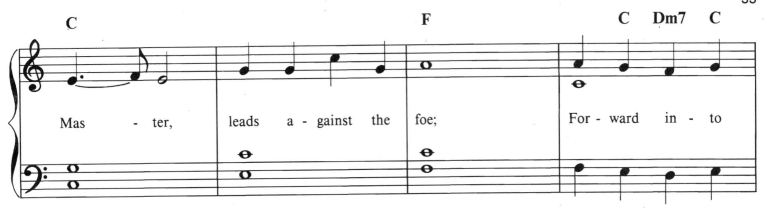

Mas - ter, leads a - gainst the foe; For - ward in - to

bat - tle, ____ see His ban - ners go!

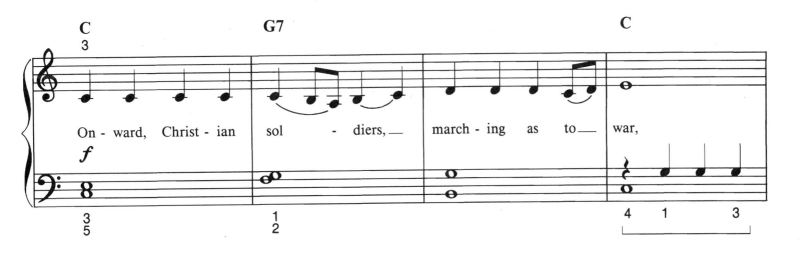

On - ward, Christ - ian sol - diers, ____ march - ing as to ____ war,

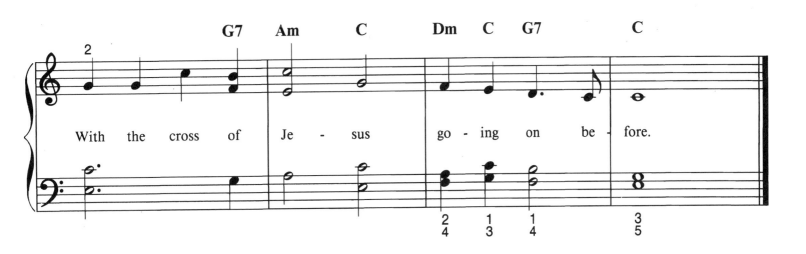

With the cross of Je - sus go - ing on be - fore.

PRAISE TO THE LORD, THE ALMIGHTY

Stately

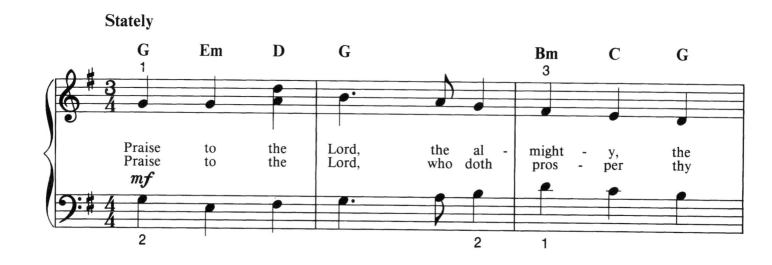

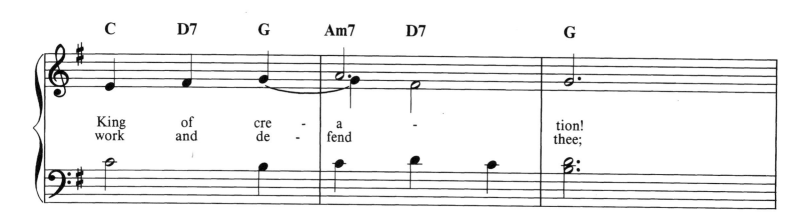

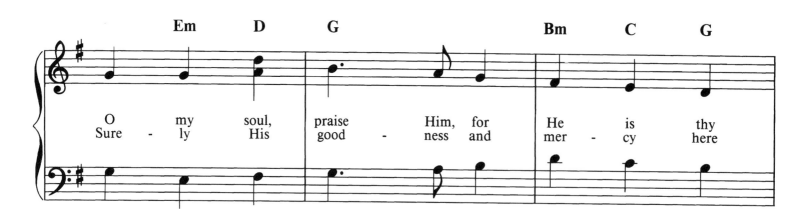

Copyright © 1986 HAL LEONARD PUBLISHING CORPORATION
International Copyright Secured   ALL RIGHTS RESERVED   Printed in the U.S.A.

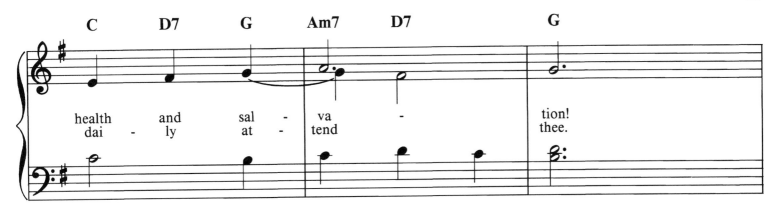

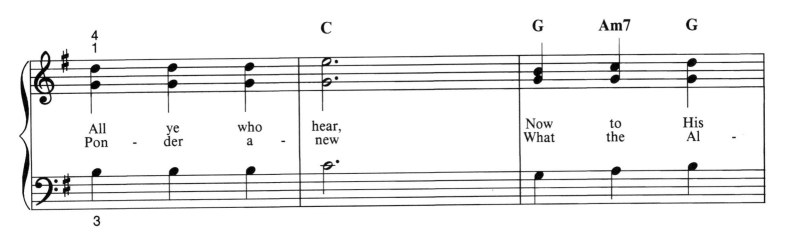

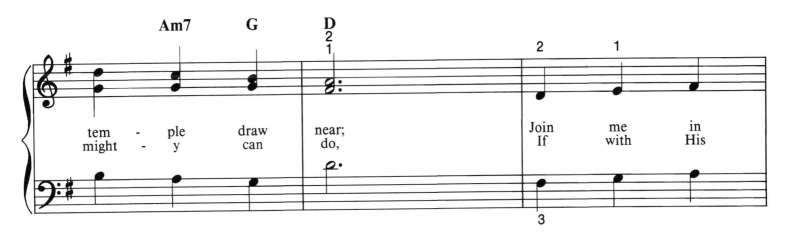

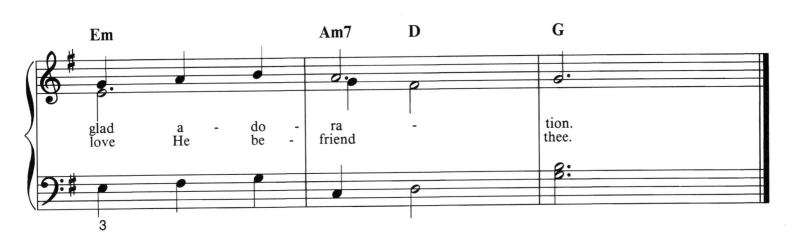

PRECIOUS MEMORIES

Moderately slow

Pre - cious mem - 'ries,   un - seen an - gels
Pre - cious fa - ther,   lov - ing moth - er

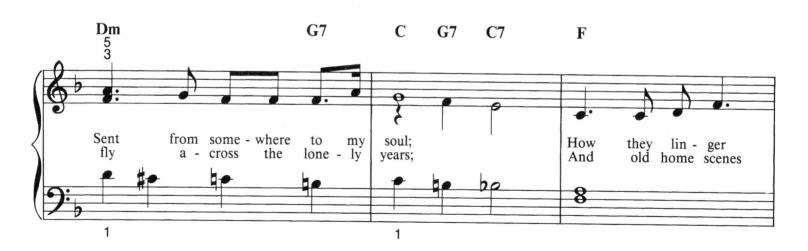

Sent   from some - where to my   soul;   How   they lin - ger
fly   a - cross the lone - ly   years;   And   old home scenes

Copyright © 1986 HAL LEONARD PUBLISHING CORPORATION
International Copyright Secured   ALL RIGHTS RESERVED   Printed in the U.S.A

ev - er near me / And the sa - cred past un - fold.
of my child - hood / In fond mem - o - ry ap - pears.

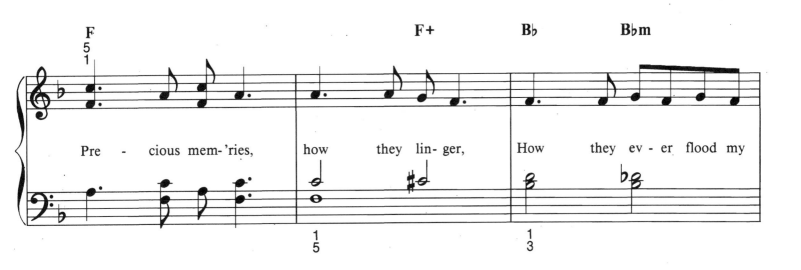

Pre - cious mem-'ries, how they lin - ger, How they ev - er flood my

soul; In the still - ness of the mid - night

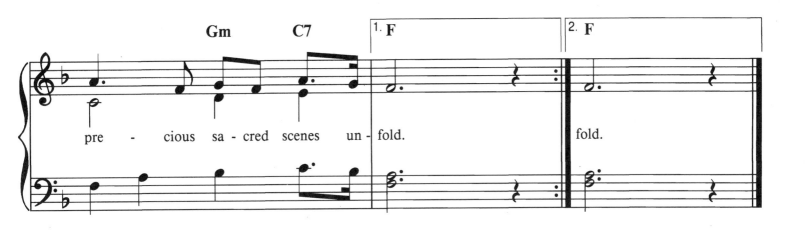

pre - cious sa - cred scenes un - fold. fold.

ROCK OF AGES, CLEFT FOR ME

Copyright © 1986 HAL LEONARD PUBLISHING CORPORATION
International Copyright Secured   ALL RIGHTS RESERVED   Printed in the U.S.A.

SWEET HOUR OF PRAYER

Copyright © 1986 HAL LEONARD PUBLISHING CORPORATION
International Copyright Secured   ALL RIGHTS RESERVED   Printed in the U.S.A.

SHALL WE GATHER AT THE RIVER?

Like a slow march

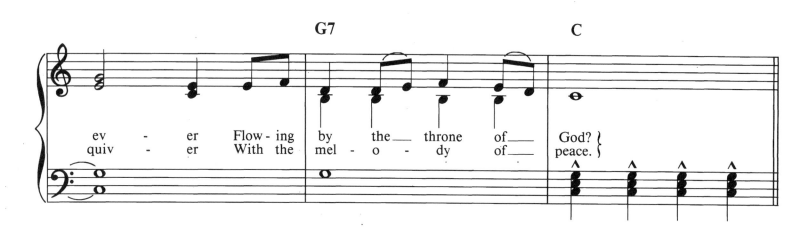

Copyright © 1986 HAL LEONARD PUBLISHING CORPORATION
International Copyright Secured   ALL RIGHTS RESERVED   Printed in the U.S.A.

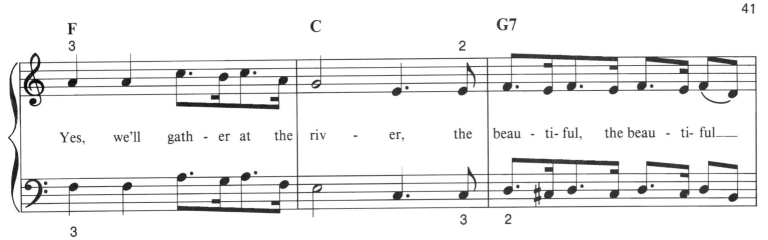

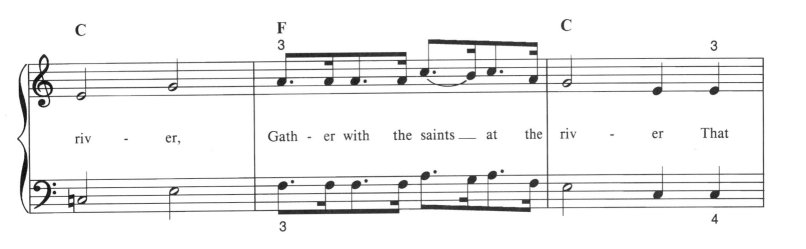

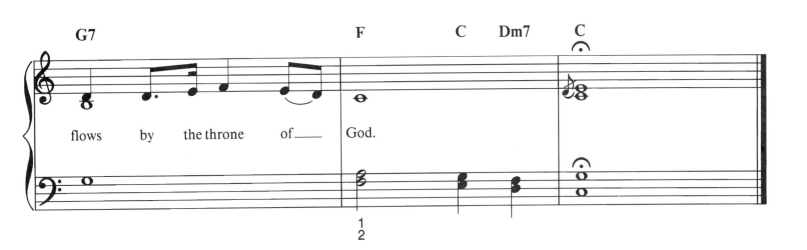

TAKE MY LIFE AND LET IT BE

Copyright © 1986 HAL LEONARD PUBLISHING CORPORATION
International Copyright Secured   ALL RIGHTS RESERVED   Printed in the U.S.A.

WE GATHER TOGETHER
TO ASK THE LORD'S BLESSING

Moderately, flowing

We gath - er to - geth - er to ask the Lord's bless - ing; He
chas - tens and has - tens His will to make known. The
wick - ed op - press - ing now cease _____ from dis - tress - ing, Sing
prais - es to His name: _____ He for - gets not His own.

Copyright © 1986 HAL LEONARD PUBLISHING CORPORATION
International Copyright Secured   ALL RIGHTS RESERVED   Printed in the U.S.A.

WERE YOU THERE?

With feeling

Copyright © 1986 HAL LEONARD PUBLISHING CORPORATION
International Copyright Secured   ALL RIGHTS RESERVED   Printed in the U.S.A.

WHEN I SURVEY
THE WONDROUS CROSS

With feeling

When I sur - vey the won - drous cross
Were I the whole realm of na - ture mine,

On which the Prince of glo - ry died,
That were a pres - ent far too small;

My rich - est gain I count but loss,
Love so a - maz - ing, so di - vine,

And pour con - tempt on all my pride.
De - mands my soul, my life, my all.

Copyright © 1986 HAL LEONARD PUBLISHING CORPORATION
International Copyright Secured   ALL RIGHTS RESERVED   Printed in the U.S.A.

WHISPERING HOPE

Copyright © 1986 HAL LEONARD PUBLISHING CORPORATION
International Copyright Secured   ALL RIGHTS RESERVED   Printed in the U.S.A.

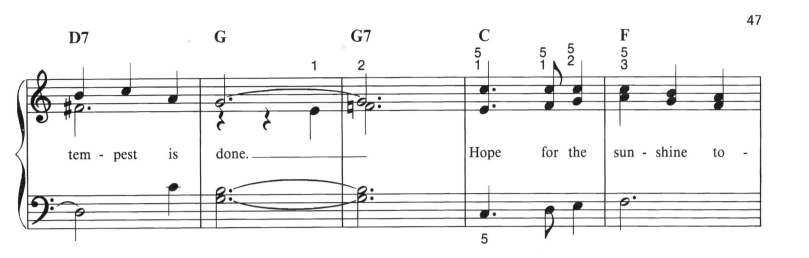

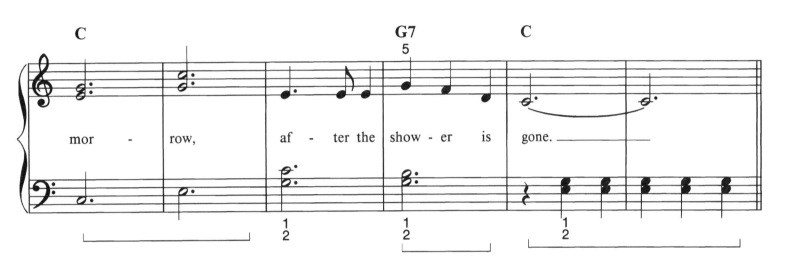

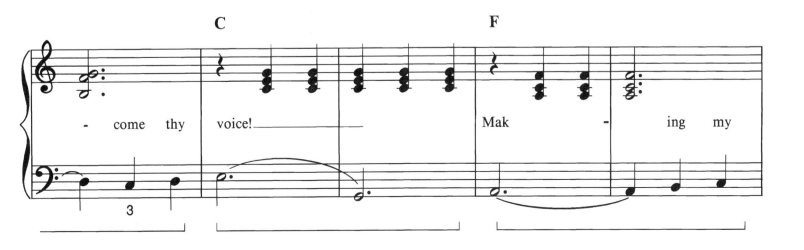